W9-BBN-004

DATE DUE

I WANT TO BE . . . BOOK SERIES
Creator/Producer: Stephanie Maze, Maze Productions
Writer and Educational Consultant: Catherine O'Neill Grace
Designer: Lisa Lytton-Smith

Photographers for I WANT TO BE AN ASTRONAUT:
Barbara Ries, Karen Kasmauski, Mike Clemmer,
Cary Wolinsky, Richard T. Nowitz

Other books in this series:
I WANT TO BE A DANCER
I WANT TO BE AN ENGINEER
I WANT TO BE A VETERINARIAN

Requests for permission to make copies
of any part of the work should be mailed to:
Permissions Department, Harcourt Brace & Company,
6277 Sea Harbor Drive, Orlando, Florida 32887-6777.

Library of Congress Cataloging-in-Publication Data
Maze, Stephanie.
I want to be an astronaut/by Stephanie Maze and Catherine O'Neill Grace
p. cm.— (I want to be . . . book series)
Summary: Describes what it is like to be an astronaut, some of the ways
to prepare for this career, and the work in various related jobs.
ISBN 0-15-201300-8
1. Astronautics—Juvenile literature. [1. Astronautics—Vocational guidance.
2. Astronauts. 3. Occupations. 4. Vocational guidance.]
I. Grace, Catherine O'Neill, 1950– . II. Title. III. Series.
TL789.2.M38 1997
629.45'023—dc20 96-17481

First edition
C E F D B

Pre-press through PrintNet
Printed and bound by Tien Wah Press, Singapore

I Want to Be...

AN ASTRONAUT

A Maze Productions Book

HARCOURT BRACE & COMPANY

SAN DIEGO   NEW YORK   LONDON

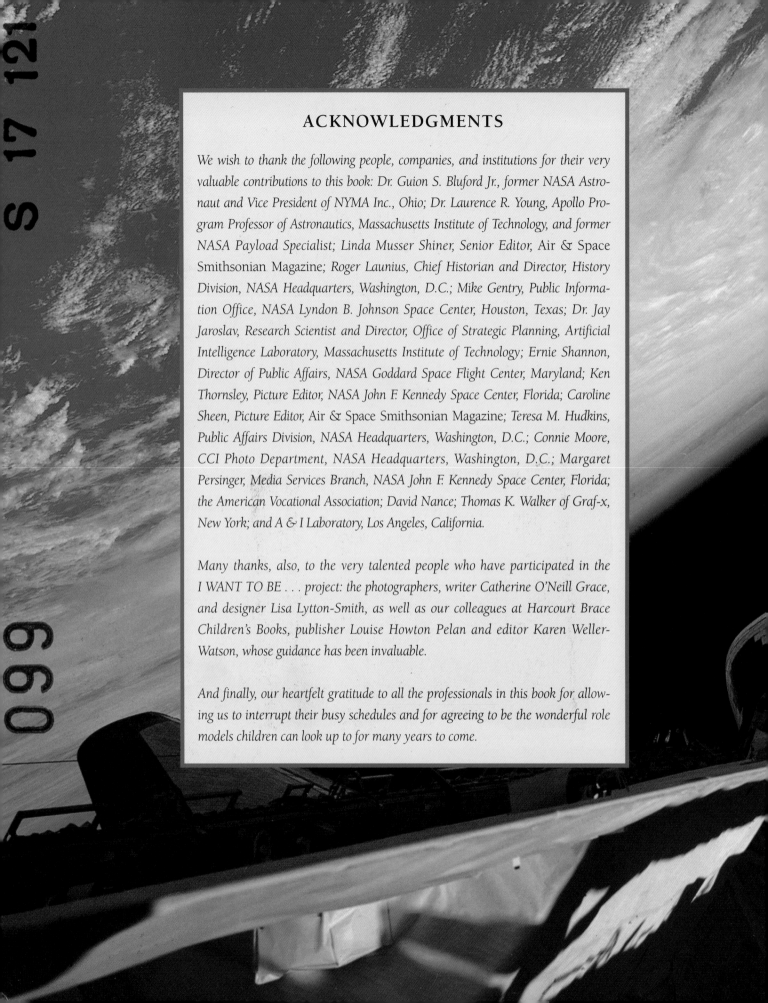

ACKNOWLEDGMENTS

We wish to thank the following people, companies, and institutions for their very valuable contributions to this book: Dr. Guion S. Bluford Jr., former NASA Astronaut and Vice President of NYMA Inc., Ohio; Dr. Laurence R. Young, Apollo Program Professor of Astronautics, Massachusetts Institute of Technology, and former NASA Payload Specialist; Linda Musser Shiner, Senior Editor, Air & Space Smithsonian Magazine; Roger Launius, Chief Historian and Director, History Division, NASA Headquarters, Washington, D.C.; Mike Gentry, Public Information Office, NASA Lyndon B. Johnson Space Center, Houston, Texas; Dr. Jay Jaroslav, Research Scientist and Director, Office of Strategic Planning, Artificial Intelligence Laboratory, Massachusetts Institute of Technology; Ernie Shannon, Director of Public Affairs, NASA Goddard Space Flight Center, Maryland; Ken Thornsley, Picture Editor, NASA John F. Kennedy Space Center, Florida; Caroline Sheen, Picture Editor, Air & Space Smithsonian Magazine; Teresa M. Hudkins, Public Affairs Division, NASA Headquarters, Washington, D.C.; Connie Moore, CCI Photo Department, NASA Headquarters, Washington, D.C.; Margaret Persinger, Media Services Branch, NASA John F. Kennedy Space Center, Florida; the American Vocational Association; David Nance; Thomas K. Walker of Graf-x, New York; and A & I Laboratory, Los Angeles, California.

Many thanks, also, to the very talented people who have participated in the I WANT TO BE . . . project: the photographers, writer Catherine O'Neill Grace, and designer Lisa Lytton-Smith, as well as our colleagues at Harcourt Brace Children's Books, publisher Louise Howton Pelan and editor Karen Weller-Watson, whose guidance has been invaluable.

And finally, our heartfelt gratitude to all the professionals in this book for allowing us to interrupt their busy schedules and for agreeing to be the wonderful role models children can look up to for many years to come.

To all children who dream the impossible dreams

Where to Start

Can you picture yourself in a space suit? Do you dream about traveling in space or going to other planets? Can you imagine climbing aboard a space shuttle?

Astronauts Bernard A. Harris and C. Michael Foale had dreams like yours that came true. The astronauts blasted off on the space shuttle *Discovery* in 1995. In this picture, Harris (top) and Foale are on their way out of the shuttle orbiter for some extravehicular activity (EVA). This means that they're getting ready to leave the vehicle for a space walk, protected by their high-tech space suits.

Harris was payload commander and Foale was a mission specialist on the flight. Payload crew members are scientists or engineers who run and analyze experiments during a mission. Mission specialists are technical/scientific astronauts who also run experiments in flight and work with the pilots to keep the shuttle running smoothly.

Whether you hope to fly the shuttle or to supervise experiments on board, taking math and science courses now will help you prepare. These two astronauts studied hard to get into the space program. Harris earned a doctorate of medicine at Texas Tech. Foale earned a doctorate in astrophysics from Cambridge University in England.

Education is essential for astronauts. Fields in which they train include mathematics, astronomy, engineering, geology, chemistry, biology, physics, and electronics. Although you don't have to be a championship athlete, fitness is important, too. You must be in top physical condition to go into space, so prepare your body with healthful food and exercise.

Looking Back at Earth

If you ever travel into space, you will be able to gaze back at our planet and see the many shapes and patterns on Earth's surface. Until then, take a look at these "postcards" from shuttle missions. Cameras aboard spacecraft have recorded thousands of detailed images of our planet. In the background of the facing page, pale shades of blue reveal shallow lagoons around the Bahamas. The dark blue shows channels between the islands that plunge one to two thousand miles deep.

The smaller images above provide other views of our planet's diverse geography. At left is an infrared image of a river delta on the island of Madagascar. It records how years of heavy erosion have filled in the waterway. The center image shows the peaks of the Andes range in Argentina, in South America. The shot was made with a handheld camera from the space shuttle *Atlantis*. In the third picture above, you can see a vast area of sand dunes in the Sahara Desert.

The nose of the space shuttle *Atlantis* is silhouetted against a half-globe portrait of Earth, at far right. The photograph was taken when the U.S. shuttle was docked at the Russian Mir space station in 1995.

Imagine what kinds of images will come back to Earth from spacecraft in the twenty-first century!

Living in Space

In space you have to take care of yourself as you do on Earth—but it's more difficult. At right, astronaut William B. Lenoir, an electrical engineer by training, tries his hand at being a barber. He trims the sideburns of space shuttle *Columbia*'s pilot, Robert F. Overmyer, during a mission in 1982. Aboard *Endeavour* in 1992, Japanese astronaut Mamoru Mohri lathers up for a dry shampoo.

Washing your hair, brushing your teeth, having a snack, going to the bathroom, getting some exercise, or taking a snooze all sound like ordinary things to do, don't they? How about performing all those daily tasks while you're weightless—and the tools you need to use are weightless, too? That's the challenge astronauts deal with every day while they're on a mission. They use lots of straps to hold things down. Even the toilet has a seatbelt!

Of course, weightlessness can be fun. Sometimes astronauts fool around a bit when they're relaxing during a mission. Astronauts Daniel W. Bursch and Frank L. Culbertson did as they brushed their teeth before going to bed aboard the space shuttle *Discovery* one evening in 1993. No, Culbertson isn't standing on his head. He's floating upside down! In the background you can see sleep restraints attached to the wall. The straps will keep the astronauts from floating around the cabin while they're sleeping.

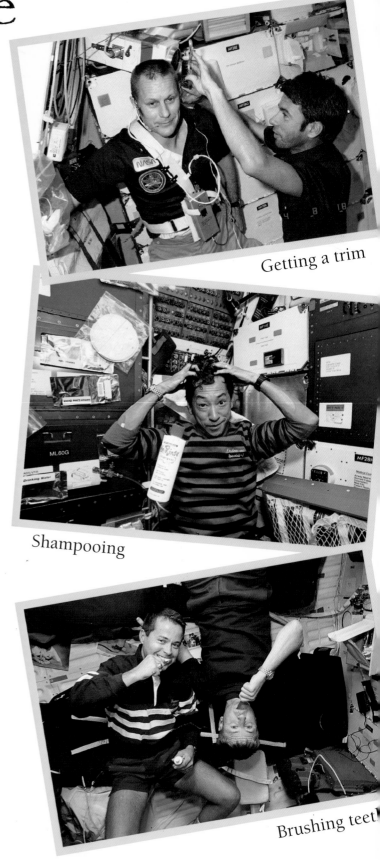

Getting a trim

Shampooing

Brushing teeth

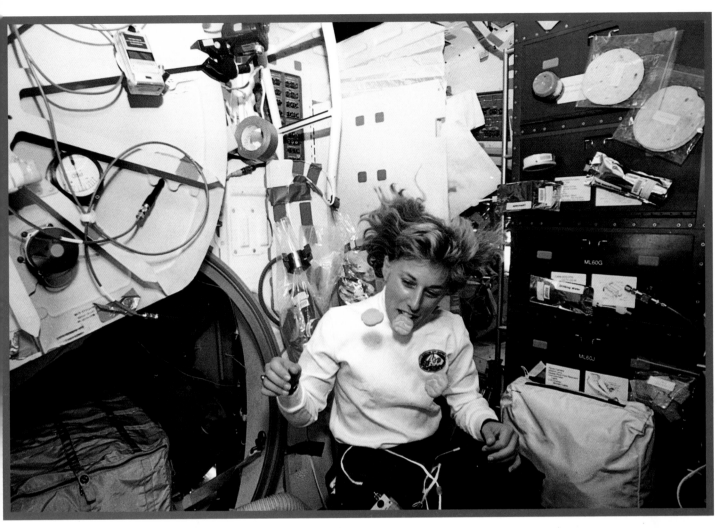

Pass the cookies! *Mission specialist Jan Davis, a biologist and mechanical engineer, goes after some floating Girl Scout goodies on* Endeavour *in 1992. The flight was the fiftieth U.S. shuttle mission.*

Soccer and snoozing. *On* Discovery, *John E. Blaha tosses a ball. At far right,* Challenger *astronauts Richard H. Truly and Guion S. Bluford Jr. nap.*

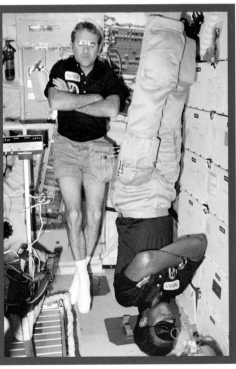

Training to Be an Astronaut

It takes many years of training to become an astronaut. After they are selected, astronauts-to-be train at facilities in Texas, Alabama, and Florida. At the Weightless Environment Training Facility, part of the Lyndon B. Johnson Space Center in Houston, trainees like mission specialist Leroy Chiao (small photo above) learn everything they need to know to do their extravehicular jobs correctly in zero-gravity conditions in space. Above, astronauts-in-training wearing extravehicular mobility units (EMUs)—the suits that make it possible to survive outside a spacecraft—practice for the Hubble Space Telescope repair mission. They may look as if they're in space but they're not. The bubbles—and the diver in the background—are clear signals that they are underwater. Working conditions in the giant pool are like those that the astronauts would find in space. This helps them learn how to maneuver and to use tools in the bulky space suits.

Trips in a modified jet airplane give astronauts-in-training a chance to actually experience the feeling of weightlessness—if only for a few seconds. The airplane produces weightlessness by diving from thirty-five thousand to twenty-four thousand feet. *Zoom!* People inside are weightless for about twenty seconds during the dive. One of the side effects of this training is airsickness. Some astronauts feel queasy in weightless conditions during missions in space, too. But they get used to it and feel better after a while. During training, the nose dives may be repeated as often as forty times in one day. Riding a roller coaster must seem pretty tame after that!

I'm flying! *Aboard a KC 135 aircraft executing a nearly two-mile dive (above), payload specialists laugh as they experience what it's like to be weightless.*

Just as important is practicing the checklist run-through in a shuttle cockpit simulator, as Charles F. Bolden Jr. and NASA's Steven A. Nesbitt are doing below.

Astronauts prepare for many different situations they might encounter if their craft landed somewhere other than at a fully equipped space center. Above, astronaut Mae C. Jemison—who in 1992 became the first African American woman in space when she flew on the space shuttle *Endeavour*—takes part in land survival training. Astronaut candidates learn parachute jumping, scuba diving, and sea survival skills, too. When they finally lift off, they are ready to deal with just about anything.

Experiments in Space

Astronauts come from all walks of life. They are doctors and scientists, politicians and pilots, teachers and vets, engineers and authors. All have many responsibilities when they're out in space. They work very hard. A space workday may last sixteen hours—twice as long as a typical workday back on Earth.

Space shuttle crews perform many jobs. Some deliver equipment, such as satellites and telescopes, and others go into space to repair craft that are already out there. Sometimes they pick up equipment from space or they give other astronauts lifts back to Earth. That's what happened when *Atlantis* docked at the Russian station, Mir.

Astronauts often use their time to look back and study Earth to learn about pollution, geography, and weather patterns. They observe the stars and planets, too. And they conduct scientific experiments—especially when Spacelab, an extra cabin that's equipped as a high-tech science laboratory, is on board.

Certain experiments investigate the effects of microgravity on humans, animals, insects, and plants. In the picture top right, an astronaut checks to see how some moths are responding to the zero gravity of space.

Other experiments test whether new products can be made in space that would be useful back home.

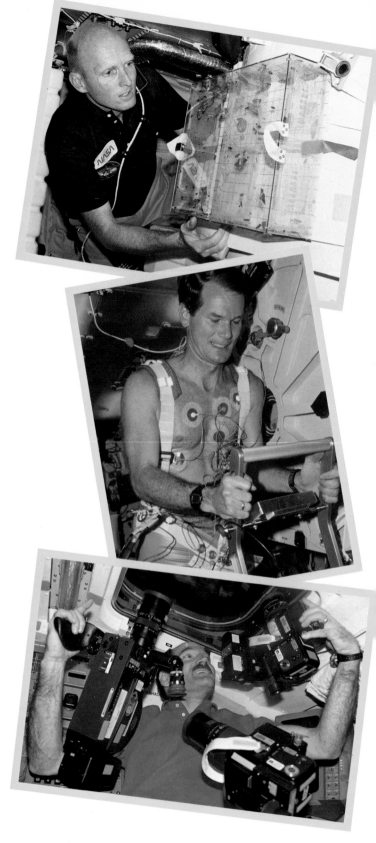

C. Gordon Fullerton checks moth experiment (top). Medical research occupies Congressman Bill Nelson, using a treadmill on Columbia (middle). On Atlantis (bottom), Guy S. Gardner tries to keep his weightless cameras orga-

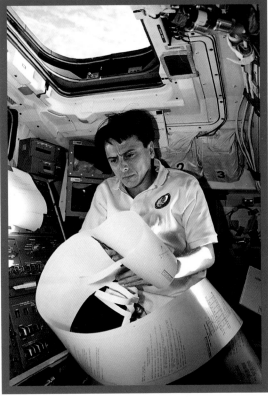

nized . Marsha S. Ivins, an engineer, records heat images of Earth as Pierre J. Thuot assists (top). Physician Rhea Seddon and veterinarian Martin J. Fettman study weightlessness (above). Physicist Franklin R. Chang-Diaz struggles with a l-o-n-g message from home (right).

Space Walks

Here on Earth all you need to do to take a walk is put on your shoes and head down the street. In space it's more complicated. Astronauts start putting on their gear several hours before space walks. Their suits are life-support systems that protect them from the environment outside the spacecraft. The space suit is equipped with an extravehicular mobility unit (EMU) to provide power for moving around. The suit also protects its wearer from the extreme hot and cold temperatures in space and against the vacuum and radiation of space and the chance of getting hit by micrometeorites. It provides air to breathe, a waste collection device so the astronaut does not need a bathroom, and a communications system. Food and water are also stored in it.

Edward H. White was the first astronaut to perform extravehicular activity (EVA). His feat—the first space walk—occurred in June 1965 and lasted twenty-three minutes. Since then astronauts have completed dozens of EVAs, which never get boring.

Spacewalking equipment
has become more and
more sophisticated since
Ed White left Gemini 4
tethered to his spacecraft
with a lifeline (inset, top
left). By 1984 Bruce
McCandless II could pull
away from Challenger
using foot restraints
(second inset from top).
In 1991, from Discovery,
McCandless was the first
astronaut to use a
manned maneuvering
unit (MMU), which
enables the user to move
freely (third inset from
top). At bottom left, F.
Story Musgrave prepares
to install equipment on
the Hubble Space
Telescope. In the large
picture on this page,
Mark C. Lee tests a
rescue system for space-
walkers. At far left, Dale
A. Gardner, his work of
recovering a satellite
done, holds up a FOR
SALE sign. Don't worry,
mission control. It was
just a joke!

Education and Training

You don't have to wait until college to learn more about space science. Tell your teacher or principal about the National Aeronautics and Space Administration's (NASA) Teacher Resource Centers, a nonprofit program that provides videotapes, slides, computer software, and other materials about the space program to schools. Many spaceflight centers, universities, and science-and-technology museums offer hands-on programs for kids. Top right, students from E. Brooke Lee Middle School in Silver Spring, Maryland, try on a space suit at NASA's Goddard Space Flight Center in Maryland. Goddard was the first major U.S. spaceflight lab. It has been operating since 1959. Other students at Patrick Henry Elementary School in Arlington, Virginia (second from top), build space satellites with aluminum foil in class. They are participants in the Young Astronauts program.

Young Astronauts is a national program headquartered in Minnesota. It offers schools around the country a challenging and fun space curriculum that covers astronomy, flight, rocketry, shuttle missions, and life in space. At right (third from top), ninth graders at Montgomery Blair High School in Silver Spring, Maryland, learn the fundamentals of physics by building a catapult to launch coins.

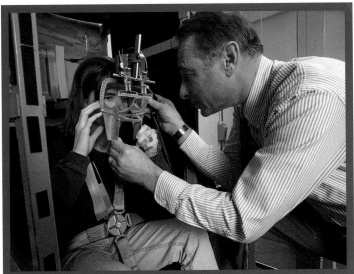

Hands-on science. *At Kennedy Space Center in Florida, University High School students from Orlando make last-minute adjustments to a model shuttle (far left, bottom). In large photo above, a military pilot trains in an F-16 cockpit simulator at General Dynamics in Fort Worth, Texas. Many astronauts enter the space program through military training. Above right, student Liana Lorigo manipulates a lunar robot, which she built at the Massachusetts Institute of Technology's Artificial Intelligence Lab. Above left, Dr. Larry Young, Apollo Program professor of Astronautics at MIT and a former NASA payload specialist, helps a student from MIT's Man-Vehicle Lab adjust her mask as she sits on a "sled" used to study motion and visual perception in space.*

Learning Programs

Going to camp means doing crafts, swimming, sitting around a fire and telling ghost stories . . . right? Not at space camp. There you try out astronaut water survival training, launch your own model rocket, and take part in a simulated space shuttle mission.

There are several space camps in the United States. Two of the best known camps are located at the U.S. Space and Rocket Center in Huntsville, Alabama, and in Florida near NASA's Kennedy Space Center. At space camp you learn about the space program and the science of spaceflight. But the programs involve more than that. Space camps focus on teamwork and problem-solving ability, too—skills astronauts need.

Students in Charleston, South Carolina, who got involved with NASA's Can Do program actually launched experiments into space. Their experiments were loaded into one of the shuttles' "Get Away Special" (GAS) cans, which NASA provides for special educational and research purposes. Their work went into space aboard the space shuttle *Endeavour* in 1993.

Take a look. *Second graders at Mary Ford Elementary School in Charleston, South Carolina, examine images of Africa's Zaire River that were made with a camera other students sent aloft aboard* Endeavour *(top). Above, high school students at NASA's Ames Research Center in Mountain View, California, wear special glasses to observe heat patterns from sources out in the universe. At right, in Huntsville, Alabama, space campers try out a mission control station, a reduced-gravity chair, and a spacewalk simulator.*

Challenger Learning Center

In 1986 the space shuttle *Challenger* exploded seventy-three seconds after blastoff. Seven astronauts— among them Christa McAuliffe, the first teacher to prepare for spaceflight—died. After the disaster the families of the seven astronauts did not turn their backs on the space program. Instead, they founded an education program in memory of the *Challenger* crew.

The program, called the Challenger Center, uses space exploration to get kids excited about science, math, and technology. It also encourages young people to pursue careers that use those skills—like becoming an astronaut.

The Challenger Center experience begins in the classroom. Student crews prepare for a simulation of a space mission. They do team assignments in navigation, communication, life support, and space-probe assembly.

The mission itself takes place at one of twenty-five learning centers located in science museums, schools, and other educational institutions throughout the United States and Canada—including the Challenger Research,

Development & Training Center in Washington, D.C., shown on these pages. During their simulated spaceflights, students may launch a space probe into the tail of a comet, land on the Moon, relieve a research team stationed on Mars, or study Earth's environment from space. Student crews work in mission control and aboard a model spacecraft. It's very realistic!

The students in these photographs go to Bailey Elementary School for the Arts and Sciences in Fairfax, Virginia. At left, classmates John Paez and Michael Osorto work with a glove-box laboratory that's free of contaminants. They're examining rocks and other substances for radioactivity and magnetism. Meanwhile, Trang Phan (far left), wearing a headset, serves as a communications officer, linking the space station with mission control.

The thousands of young people who take part in Challenger Center programs every year share the mission of astronauts on *Challenger*'s last flight—to learn, to explore, and to inspire.

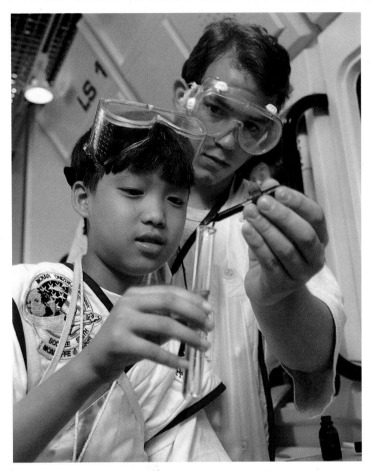

Life-support officers Phuc Nguyen and William Lowrey are in charge of the astronauts' safety. Above, they test drinking water for solvents.

Below, Maria Ibarra checks Jacqueline Zacatales's blood pressure. In space, astronauts monitor their bodies—so Challenger Center students do, too.

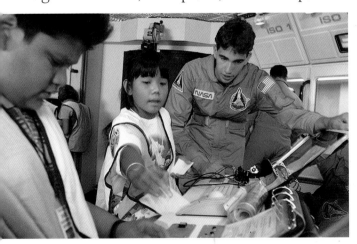

The shuttle flight deck is command central during a simulated mission. Above, communications officer Trang Phan unloads data from a computer.

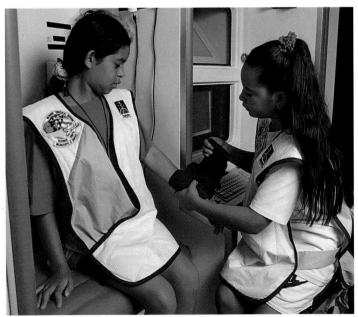

Launch Support Staff

Have you watched a shuttle launch? As the craft lifts off, do you wonder who built it? Do you try to figure out how they move something that size onto the launchpad? (The shuttle weighs about a hundred tons without booster rockets!)

Getting the shuttle and its crew ready for a mission is a team effort that goes on for months before the launch. The NASA photographs on these pages show some of the people behind the scenes. At the Orbiter Processing Facility at the Kennedy Space Center (left), *Endeavour* is lifted into vertical position so that the fuel tank and booster rockets can be connected. Technicians install shuttle engines in the photo inset at far left. Another Orbiter Processing Facility expert inspects fuel lines (inset, near left). Members of the support staff also help astronauts prepare for their work in space. Technicians assist astronaut Sherwood C. Spring during training in the KC 135 zero-gravity aircraft (top right). At the Weightlessness Environment Training Center in Houston, Texas, astronauts George D. Nelson and John M. Lounge, clad in space suits, work underwater to simulate conditions in space; a diver helps them learn emergency techniques for repairing the shuttle (center right). Aboard the KC 135 training plane, mission specialist William F. Fisher holds a mirror as shuttle pilot C. Gordon Fullerton practices fastening important linkups on his space suit (bottom right).

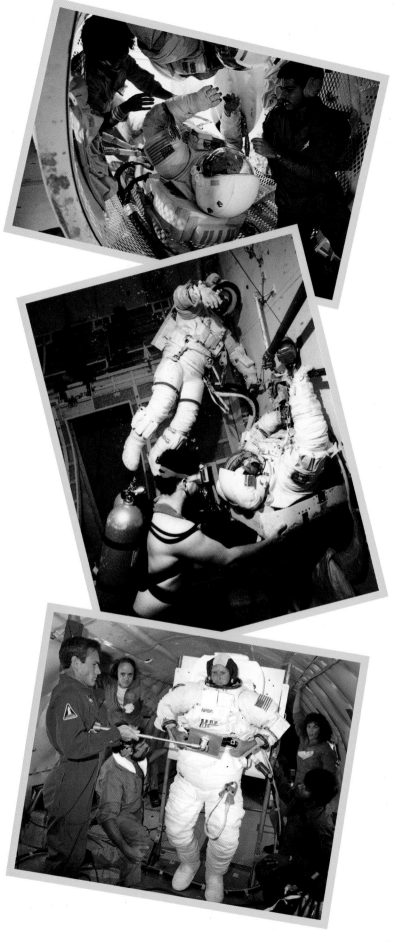

Technical Support Staff

Here on Earth, thousands of people perform millions of tasks at labs and factories all over the world with one goal in mind: to get astronauts and their payloads off the ground. This hard work supports U.S. astronauts as well as missions designed in other countries. Above, a technician installs wires in an orbiter spacecraft. At top right, in the Operations and Checkout Building at Kennedy Space Center, Italian aerospace technicians work on a satellite that will be carried aboard *Columbia* in a joint venture of NASA and the Italian space agency. In another building at the Kennedy Space Center, launch-pad workers put together a communications satellite owned by India (second from top). Carried into space aboard a *Delta* rocket, the Indian satellite was designed to aid TV broadcasts and to make weather observations. In photo third from top, a NASA quality inspector checks windows on *Endeavour*. Once spacecraft and satellites are launched, communications specialists monitor their movement. At the Goddard Space Flight Center in Maryland (bottom right), a master console controls all direct voice communications about orbiting spacecraft.

How many inspectors does it take to launch a spacecraft? *Lots! A large team of engineers and technicians in a huge, multilevel hangar at Kennedy Space Center in Florida performs a preflight checkout of the interplanetary explorer spacecraft Ulysses. The Ulysses project was a joint venture of NASA and the European Space Agency. Launched from the space shuttle Discovery in 1990, Ulysses set off on a five-year mission to explore regions of the Sun's north and south poles. Ulysses was one of many interplanetary probes. Magellan, which sped toward Venus, and Galileo, sent to explore Jupiter, were launched in 1989.*

International Space Partners

Atlantis, meet Mir! On June 29, 1995, U.S. space shuttle *Atlantis* commander Robert L. Gibson made history as he carefully docked his craft at the Russian Mir space station, 245 miles out in space.

It was a tricky maneuver, but Gibson did it perfectly. *Atlantis* and Mir were both traveling through space at 17,500 miles per hour, and Gibson had only a four-minute window to perform the docking. The photograph of Mir above was made as *Atlantis* approached the space station. The small picture at left shows what *Atlantis* looked like from Mir.

Cheers went up on Earth—in Russia as well as the United States—as Gibson told mission control, "Houston, we have capture!" After fourteen years, the shuttle was doing what its designers had planned: connecting with another craft in space. Linked together, the

wo created a craft as big as a fifteen-story
uilding—the largest structure ever assembled
n space. The historic Mir/*Atlantis* mission
nade more real the dream of establishing large
nternational research stations in space from
vhich people can travel back and forth.

After the docking, the shuttle crew moved
hrough an airlock that connects the shuttle
vith the orbiter docking system. Then shuttle
rew members crossed into Mir and floated
long a passageway to reach the Mir crew.

The two Russian cosmonauts and one
american astronaut on board Mir, who had

All together now! *Russian cosmonaut Gennadi Strekalov takes a break from serious duties to strum his guitar and sing, accompanied by NASA astronauts Bonnie J. Dunbar, Gregory Harbaugh, and pilot Charles Precourt (on Strekalov's right). The Russians and Americans spent five days together on Mir space station in 1995.*

een in space for 115 days, were delighted to
ee the five NASA astronauts and two Russian
osmonauts from *Atlantis*. There were hugs all
round.

All ten space explorers posed for a historic
ortrait (above). The members of the group
pent five days conducting biomedical
esearch—and getting to know each other
etter. Members of the group traveled home
o Earth aboard the space shuttle *Atlantis*.

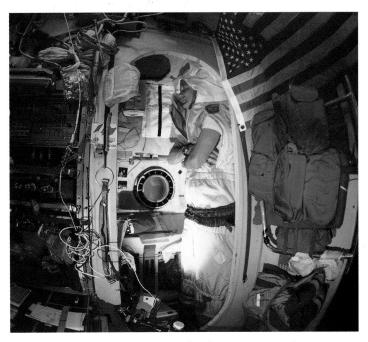

Sleep tight. *Norman Thagard, who spent 115 days on Mir with two Russian cosmonauts before* Atlantis *arrived to pick them up, is zipped into his sleep restraint for one more night a long way from home.*

Astronaut Vocabulary

Like any technical work, being an astronaut requires knowing lots of unusual words. The space program does such new things that it has to invent a new vocabulary to go with them! On these pages, you'll learn some important space words and concepts.

MATING

Mating is the term used when an orbiter is connected to the external fuel tank and solid rocket boosters that will propel it into space. This happens inside the Vehicle Assembly Building at Kennedy Space Center in Florida. Here, the orbiter *Discovery* is slowly being moved from a horizontal to a vertical position for the mating.

INTERPLANETARY PROBE

Galileo is an interplanetary probe that was launched in 1989 from a cradlelike device aboard the space shuttle *Atlantis*. From there, this spacecraft began a six-year journey to the planet Jupiter. *Galileo* will not return, but it transmits information back to Earth about things in deep space that have never been seen before.

LAUNCH

The launch of a spacecraft is the act of propelling it from Earth, through our atmosphere, and into space. Getting into orbit is the hardest part of a launch. A rocket must be traveling nearly eighteen thousand miles per hour to do it. Here, two powerful rockets help provide thrust to launch a shuttle.

ORBITER

The shuttle plane—the part of the space shuttle that is launched into space by powerful booster rockets, circles Earth, and then glides home to land like an airplane on a runway—is called an orbiter. This photograph shows the orbiter *Challenger* gliding far above Earth during a mission in 1983.

DOCKING MODULE

When an orbiter approaches a space station, it is equipped with a docking module like this one, built by the Russian space program. Shuttle pilots use docking modules to link their ships to space stations. Mission Commander Robert L. Gibson used this module in 1995 when he parked *Atlantis* at the Russian Mir space station.

FERRYING

An orbiter has no power of its own to fly through our atmosphere. After it glides in from space and lands, the orbiter is mounted on a Boeing 747 aircraft to be returned to Kennedy Space Center so it can be used again. This piggyback method of transportation is called ferrying.

SPACE SHUTTLE FLIGHT DECK

These are the complex controls, computerized displays, and communications systems that a shuttle crew must be able to read and use in order to fly the spacecraft. This photograph shows the forward space shuttle flight deck console on *Endeavour.*

SPACE SUIT

Space suits are life-support systems that astronauts wear when they go outside the spacecraft. This model space suit is an AX-5. It is being tested for use outside NASA's future space station. Space suits contain air to breathe and keep the body at the right temperature.

SPACE TELESCOPE

Space shuttles have launched many telescopes to look far out into deep space. The Hubble, shown here, is one of the most remarkable— although astronauts had to spend more than a week in space repairing it! This huge space telescope has transmitted breathtaking images of space phenomena never before seen.

SPACELAB

Some shuttle missions carry a fully equipped science laboratory into space for conducting all kinds of carefully controlled experiments. This special cabin is called Spacelab. It also includes external equipment for mounting telescopes and other scientific instruments.

Did You Know . . .

. . . that the two solid rocket boosters and three main engines, supplied with fuel from the external tank, provided nearly seven million pounds of thrust (or force) to launch the shuttle *Discovery* (right) on mission STS-64 from Kennedy Space Center on September 9, 1994? That the boosters use up all their propellant two minutes after launch, then are released from the orbiter and descend by parachute into the ocean, where they are retrieved by special ships, and are used again for other shuttle missions? But that the fuel tank will separate about eight minutes after liftoff and disintegrate into the atmosphere, never to be seen again?

. . . that the first man-made object to orbit Earth was *Sputnik 1,* launched by the Soviet Union in 1957?

. . . that the footprints astronauts left on the Moon are still there? That's because there's no atmosphere on the Moon and therefore no wind currents to blow the prints away.

. . . that toilets on spacecraft look like the ones in your house but use spinning air instead of water to flush out waste?

. . . that there is a moon rock set in a stained-glass window at the National Cathedral in Washington, D.C.?

. . . that the outside of the space shuttle reaches a temperature of 2,300 degrees Fahrenheit as it reenters Earth's atmosphere?

. . . that the *Voyager* space probes, launched in 1977, carry music and greetings in various languages, as well as pictures of a man, a woman, and a child?

. . . that astronauts grow taller in space because their bones are not compressed together the way they are in Earth's gravity?

. . . that there are hundreds of pieces of "space junk," like pieces of old satellites, in orbit around Earth?

. . . that spiders sent into space on the shuttle were confused by weightlessness at first but still quickly figured out how to weave webs?

High Tech

Keeping track of all the satellites, telescopes, space probes, and shuttle missions that travel beyond our atmosphere is a big job. It's coordinated by the NASA Communications System (NASCOM), headquartered at Goddard Space Flight Center in Maryland. Goddard is the center of a network of information-monitoring and -processing stations that circle the globe. There are major NASCOM switching centers in Australia, Spain, and the United States, as well as many smaller tracking stations around the world. During shuttle missions, technicians at the spaceflight centers in Florida and Texas get into the act, too.

As a spacecraft moves above the ground-based tracking stations, engineers and technicians use high-tech equipment to watch and listen to the craft passing overhead. Then the next station in the system picks it up, and so on. . . .

Monitoring of space goes on twenty-four hours a day, 365 days a year. At right, technicians at the Jet Propulsion Laboratory in Pasadena, California, track unmanned space probes exploring the planets in deep space. Here, they're receiving information from a Jupiter mission.

Earth-space links. In the small picture at far right, a technician operates a voice control console at the Goddard Communications Command Center. Ground controllers at mission control in Houston, Texas, use computers to track a shuttle in inset photo above.

Home sweet space. *A shuttle is docked at the International Space Station in this computer-generated illustration. In the photo inset above, three astronauts explore a model of a habitation module that's a lot like the one the space station will contain.*

International Space Station

When the space shuttle *Atlantis* docked with space station Mir in 1995, history was made. Someday events like that may be more commonplace. Construction of the International Space Station—shown here in an image created by a computer—is scheduled to begin in 1997. It is supposed to be finished in 2002.

Building the space station—which is a cooperative venture of the European Space Agency, the United States, Russia, Canada, Japan, and other nations—will involve dozens of trips into space. It's impossible to transport on one mission all the parts needed to build the giant station. When it's finished, the International Space Station will be about the length and width of one and a half football fields. It will contain seven laboratories and a "habitation module" with a kitchen, a bathroom, a sleeping area, and medical equipment. A crew of six will operate the station, using power generated by huge photovoltaic panels that absorb energy from the Sun. The cells can be seen on the long "arms" of the space station (left). How much will all this travel and construction cost? A very rough estimate projects that the bill will come to sixty *billion* dollars—at least.

A History of People in Space

LAIKA
This dog was the first living creature to orbit Earth, in 1957. The Soviet Union sent her into space.

HAM
This chimpanzee was sent aloft by the United States in 1961. He came back safely.

YURI A. GAGARIN
This Soviet cosmonaut became the first man in space in April 1961.

Throughout history people have stared up into the night sky and wondered, *What's out there?*

For centuries astronomers made star charts and built observatories and telescopes to explore the mysteries of space. But they had no way to travel outside Earth's atmosphere. Only in this century have we begun to actually visit space to answer that question.

The modern space age began on October 4, 1957, when a small, ball-shaped satellite called *Sputnik 1* was launched by the Soviet Union. On October 11, 1958, a little more than a year later, NASA launched the unmanned *Pioneer 1*. This craft sent back forty-three hours of data about magnetic fields around Earth.

The space race had begun. (That's what people in the 1950s and '60s called the fierce competition between the United States and the Soviet Union to be the first nation to reach the Moon.)

The years that followed were very, very busy ones for space science. In April 1961, Yuri A. Gagarin, a Soviet cosmonaut, became the first human in space. He orbited Earth once in a small spacecraft called *Vostok 1*. The flight lasted 108 minutes.

Gagarin wasn't the first living being from Earth to venture into space, however. That honor goes to a little dog named Laika (at top left), sent into orbit by the Soviet Union in November 1957. Laika orbited Earth for a week.

VALENTINA TERESHKOVA
In 1963 this Soviet aviator became the world's first female astronaut.

DR. ROBERT H. GODDARD
This scientist and engineer invented the rocket combustion chamber but died in 1945, before the first launches began.

DR. WERNHER VON BRAUN
During World War II this German engineer invented the V-2 rocket. He left Germany and came to the United States to develop rockets based on V-2s.

On February 20, 1962, John Glenn Jr. became the first American to orbit Earth, aboard the *Mercury-Atlas 6*. He circled the planet three times, observing things like a giant dust storm in Africa and a sunrise and sunset—both within five hours!

In 1963 Soviet cosmonaut Valentina Tereshkova was launched into orbit, becoming the first woman in space. But even with these and other "firsts" accomplished, the space race continued. There was still a big prize out there that the Soviet Union and the United States were both working hard to win—the first landing on the Moon.

The United States got there first. On July 20, 1969, people around the world had their eyes glued to their TV screens, watching the crew members of the *Apollo 11* mission to the Moon make their landing. Six hours later the door of the lunar module, the *Eagle*, opened.

The words "That's one small step for man; one giant leap for mankind" were heard as astronaut Neil Armstrong stepped onto the surface. The *Apollo* astronauts left behind a plaque that says: "Here men from the planet Earth first set foot upon the Moon. July 1969 A.D. We came in peace for all mankind." In 1971 the Soviet Union launched the first space station, Salyut 1. The first U.S. space station, SkyLab, went up in 1973.

During these years, the experience astronauts had in space changed dramatically. The first astronauts traveled into space alone, crammed into small capsules, unable to move

APOLLO 11

The Apollo 11 crew (left)—Neil Armstrong, Michael Collins, and Edwin Aldrin Jr.—were the first astronauts to reach the Moon. Below, members of the Apollo 13 crew returned safely to Earth after an oxygen tank explosion ended their Moon mission. The first shuttle, Columbia, was launched in 1981 by Robert L. Crippen and John W. Young on mission STS-1 (bottom). Since then Sally K. Ride became the first American woman in space, on June 18, 1983, and Shannon Lucid has flown more missions than any other female astronaut (both pictured at right).

around. They stayed in space only briefly. They returned to Earth by splashing down at sea, to be retrieved by frogmen and ships.

But then, in 1981, twenty years after Yuri Gagarin's history-making orbit, the first space shuttle, *Columbia*, blasted off. That mission was the first by a craft that could go into space and return to Earth, land like a plane, and be reused for later missions. Since then, dozens of successful shuttle missions have been completed.

Inside the shuttle orbiter, large crews can work together. Crew members can move around, exercise, and perform experiments. And they stay in space for extended periods of time. Returning home, they land on a runway and walk right back onto their home planet. Yuri Gagarin would have been amazed.

In the 1980s the space program achieved more "firsts." In June 1983 Sally K. Ride became the first American woman in space. That August, Guion S. Bluford Jr. was the first African American man in space. In 1986 Franklin R. Chang-Diaz was the first Hispanic

APOLLO 13

FIRST SHUTTLE LAUNCH

ALLY K. RIDE   SHANNON LUCID   KATHRYN SULLIVAN   ELLEN OCHOA

FIRST AFRICAN AMERICAN ASTRONAUTS

Above, Kathryn Sullivan was the first woman to space-walk, in 1984, and Ellen Ochoa was the first Hispanic American woman in space, in 1993. At left, Ronald E. McNair, Guion S. Bluford Jr., and Frederick D. Gregory were the first African Americans admitted to the NASA space program, in 1978. Below, members of the Hubble Space Telescope crew are some of the most recent space adventurers.

American in space. In 1992 Mae C. Jemison was the first African American woman in space. Two years later, an event that no one would have believed was possible back in the 1950s happened: On February 3, 1994, cosmonaut Sergei Krikalev became the first Russian to travel on a U.S. shuttle.

Today, as we approach the twenty-first century, a new era in the history of human beings in space has begun. Russia and the United States, who for decades raced against each other to achieve new goals in space science and exploration, are working together on projects—such as the planned international station—that reach into the future. We're still searching for answers to that age-old question: "What's out there?"

FIRST HUBBLE TEAM

Planets and Space Phenomena

Centuries ago the ancient Greeks studied the stars. Imagine what those ancient astronomers would say if they could see the images on these pages, made with powerful space telescopes. In the 1990s astronomers—scientists who study the heavens—have been amazed by new information from the Hubble Space Telescope. For example, Hubble data have led them to change their estimate of the number of galaxies in space. Galaxies are huge groups containing hundreds of millions of stars. Astronomers now estimate that the universe holds fifty billion galaxies—ten times as many as they previously believed were out there.

MERCURY

MARS

JUPITER

SATURN

Space gallery. These images of our neighbors in Earth's solar system were made by cameras on interplanetary probes—spacecraft that travel far into deep space. Voyager 2 took the picture of Neptune, with its haze of gases, at right. Saturn's rings show clearly in an image also from Voyager 2, at left. Mariner 10 made a portrait of Mercury, top left. That's Mars, the rocky planet, above. To its right, you see the north pole of the giant planet Jupiter, largest in our solar system. At left, shadows mark craters on our Moon. And at right, the Moon blocks our Sun during a solar eclipse.

NEPTUNE

MOON

SOLAR ECLIPSE

New stars are forming from a towering cloud of gas in this image transmitted by the Hubble Space Telescope (left). Astronomers believe the gaseous pillars contain material for fifty new stars. The image of three rings of glowing gas around Supernova 1987A (below left), also from Hubble, remains a mystery to astronomers.

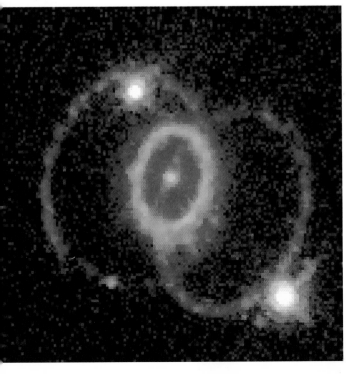

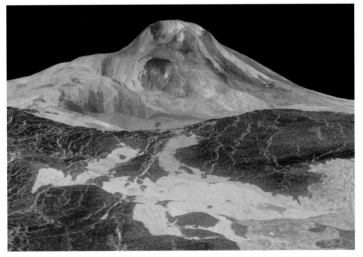

Vivid Venus. *The photo of the cloud-circled planet (top right) shows Venus. The radar image above reveals what its surface looks like. Don't let the cool color fool you— Venus's temperature averages 900 degrees Fahrenheit.*

You Can Be an Astronaut!

Suited up as astronauts at Goddard Space Flight Center, Crissy Bailey (at left in photo) and David Livingston, both from E. Brooke Lee Middle School in Silver Spring, Maryland, get a feel for the future.

In the twenty-first century, human beings will probably venture farther into space and spend more time there than ever before. Think how much remains to be explored! Perhaps these two students will be among the twenty-first-century astronauts making new discoveries to help unlock the mysteries of life in the universe. Although only a few people are selected as astronauts, there are lots of other interesting ways to have a career in space science, as you have seen in this book.

When the space program began back in the 1950s, people at NASA talked about looking for astronaut candidates who had "the right stuff." That phrase means qualities such as a spirit of adventure, technical skills, scientific curiosity, physical stamina, and bravery. Do you think you have the right stuff to become an astronaut?

Turn the page to find out where you can get more information if you want to pursue this challenging career.

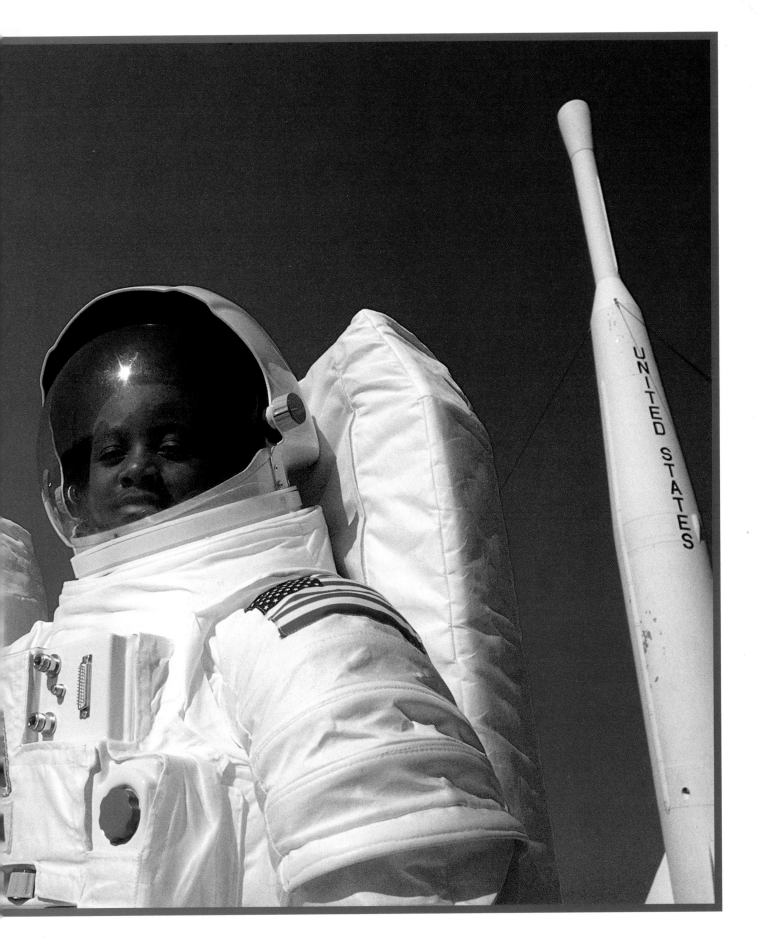

Other Sources of Information

ABOUT THE NATIONAL AERONAUTICS AND SPACE ADMINISTRATION:

NASA Headquarters
300 E Street SW
Washington, DC 20546-0001

Write for informational pamphlets and educational materials.

NASA CORE
Lorain County JVS
15181 Route 58 South
Oberlin, OH 44074

NASA's education division provides educational materials for teachers of all academic levels through NASA Teacher Resource Center Network, located at NASA research facilities and affiliated regional museums, planetariums, and universities around the country. Contact NASA CORE for a complete list.

NASA Spacelink
Marshall Space Flight Center
Mail Code CA212
Huntsville, AL 35812-0001
On the Internet:
http://spacelink.msfc.nasa.gov

A computer information service that allows individuals to receive news about current NASA programs and activities, as well as historical data about astronauts and spaceflight.

The Jet Propulsion Laboratory
Educational Affairs Office
4800 Oak Grove Drive
Pasadena, CA 91109-8099

Answers inquiries about space and planetary exploration. Houses a NASA Teacher Resource Center.

NASA SPACE CENTER VISITOR CENTERS:

NASA operates visitor centers and stages special events for the public at its major research and launch facilities around the country, including:

NASA Ames Research Center
Moffett Field, CA 94035-1000

NASA Goddard Space Flight Center
Greenbelt, MD 20771-0001

NASA Johnson Space Center
Houston, TX 77058-3696

NASA Kennedy Space Center
Kennedy Space Center, FL 32899-0001

SPACE-RELATED MUSEUMS AND VISITOR CENTERS:

Astronaut Hall of Fame
6225 Vectorspace Blvd.
Titusville, FL 32780-8040

Honors the first twenty Americans in space. Home of U.S. Space Camp, Florida.

National Air & Space Museum
Smithsonian Institution
Washington, DC 20560

The central space museum in the United States. Its Educational Resource Center can provide teachers with lesson plans, filmstrips, slides sets, computer software, and more.

U.S. Space and Rocket Center
P.O. Box 070015
Huntsville, AL 35807-7015

Full-scale shuttle display; extensive rocket collection; hands-on astronaut training exhibits; home of U.S. Space Camp, Alabama.

The Virginia Air and Space Center and Hampton Roads History Center
600 Settlers Landing Road
Hampton, VA 23669

Official visitor center for NASA Langley Research Center.

CAMPS AND LEARNING PROGRAMS:

Future Astronaut Training Program
Kansas Cosmosphere &
Space Center
1100 North Plum
Hutchison, KS 67501

Five-day summer programs for middle schoolers, designed to enhance interest in space science and related career development.

Flight Camp
Pacific Science Center
200 Second Avenue N
Seattle, WA 98109

A five-day program for space enthusiasts aged nine through twelve.

Pacific Rim Spaceflight Academy
Oregon Museum of Science
and Industry
4015 SW Canyon Road
Portland, OR 97221

*Space camp programs for ages eight
through sixteen.*

U.S. Space Camps
U.S. Space and Rocket Center
P.O. Box 070015
Huntsville, AL 35807-7015

*This group conducts camps in Alabama and Florida. Information about
both locations is available from the
address above. Ask about space camp
for grades four through seven, or
space academy for grades eight
through twelve.*

**EDUCATIONAL
ORGANIZATIONS:**

**Challenger Center for
Space Science Education**
1029 North Royal, Suite 300
Alexandria, VA 22314

*An educational organization founded
by the families of the victims of the
Challenger disaster, this group
provides innovative learning experiences through spaceflight mission
simulations for kids in grades five
through eight.*

The Young Astronaut Council
P.O. Box 65432
Washington, DC 20036
(202) 682-1984

*A private organization for elementary
and junior high school students that
creates materials and activities to
stimulate interest in science, math,
and technology. Chapters may be
formed in schools or communities.*

**ADDITIONAL SOURCES
FOR FINDING OUT
MORE ABOUT SPACE:**

Final Frontier: **The Magazine
of Space Exploration**
1516 West Lake Street
Minneapolis, MN 55408

National Space Society
922 Pennsylvania Avenue SE
Washington, DC 20003

**National Science Teachers
Association Space Science
Student Involvement Program**
5430 Roanoke Place, Suite 404
College Park, MD 20740

The Planetary Society
65 N. Catalina Ave.
Pasadena, CA 94406

**Students for the Exploration
and Development of Space**
Massachusetts Institute
of Technology
77 Massachusetts Avenue
Cambridge, MA 02139

PHOTO CREDITS